For Those Whose Lives Have Seen Themselves

poems by

Stewart Moss

Finishing Line Press
Georgetown, Kentucky

For Those Whose Lives Have Seen Themselves

For Barbara and Sara

Copyright © 2021 by Stewart Moss
ISBN 978-1-64662-557-4 First Edition
All rights reserved under International and Pan-American Copyright Conventions. No part of this book may be reproduced in any manner whatsoever without written permission from the publisher, except in the case of brief quotations embodied in critical articles and reviews.

ACKNOWLEDGMENTS

Grateful acknowledgement is made to the following publications, in whose pages these poems have appeared:

Plume Poetry Magazine ("For Those Whose Lives Have Seen Themselves;" "Hogmanay, Edinburgh;" "Holiday Candle;" "Morning Hunger;" and "The Book of Forgotten Geniuses;" and "Pas de Deux"
Origins Literary Journal
Goss 183

Special thanks to Joseph Bathanti, Grace Cavalieri, David Fountain, Danny Lawless, Claire McGoff, Leeya Mehta, Nancy Mitchell, and the late Rod Jellema—wonderful poet, brilliant teacher, and great friend. *Slainte Mhrath!*

Publisher: Leah Huete de Maines
Editor: Christen Kincaid
Cover Art: The Convex Mirror, by Harold Gresley (1892-1967), courtesy of the estate of Harold Gresley, photo by Derby Museums.
Author Photo: Stewart Moss
Cover Design: Elizabeth Maines McCleavy

Order online: www.finishinglinepress.com
also available on amazon.com

Author inquiries and mail orders:
Finishing Line Press
PO Box 1626
Georgetown, Kentucky 40324
USA

Table of Contents

A Kind of Attentiveness 1

The School Art Studio 2

A Voyeur of Refracted Light 3

Peasant Dance 4

What Is Left 5

Reading Buber 7

Aubade 8

Pas de Deux 9

How Poetry Has Let Me Down 10

Duende 11

Hogmanay, Edinburgh 12

Holiday Candle 13

For Those Whose Lives Have Seen Themselves 15

Above Tripoli 16

Fingers 18

Road Prayers in Afghanistan 20

Liberty 22

Touching the Unknown 24

Morning Hunger 26

The Sow's Dance 28

A Kind of Floating 29

When I Fell in Love with Sara, My Daughter 30

Tibetan Dress 31

The Book of Forgotten Geniuses 32

What I Want 34

A Kind of Attentiveness

What is seeing and knowing
what I see?

Is it what philosophers call
coming-into-the-nearness-of-distance,

that groping outward
breath by breath

as the quickening world
reaches forward

and grabs the quivering brain?
What is it to see a field of snow burst

into its own brilliance
then retreat into stillness,

or a splayed birch pierce the lead sky
as it melts overheard?

Ah, to be only a breathing form
with eyes and crouch, here,

forever gazing,
until my bones are bare,

arranged within the body
of the scene.

The School Art Studio

In the center is a chair
        of chipped blue enamel
shedding its paint among dismembered frames,
        old school desks scored with blood and lust,
a wobbly terra cotta jug filled
        with the dead grasses of autumn,
and a red umbrella unfastened
        dangling its nylon fronds
on the scarred oak floor.

The model's clothes are flung on the chair,
        her rumpled sweater the tallow color
of dried mulberries,
        her dungarees drawn in upon themselves,
the belt uncinched,
        its buckle grooves creeping inward
hole by hole upon an old black coat
        shiny with wear.

The evasive sun comes slatted
        through the window,
and I feel a tenderness for nakedness,
        for all the people who come and go
stepping lightly through the artifacts
        and leave their clothes as signals
like semaphores in the night.

A Voyeur of Refracted Light

Not merely metallic lakes
ablaze on melting highways,
trees shimmering in ether

or a pumpkin sun flattening
as it sinks into a sputtering sea,
or the moon's midriff bulging

above a purple arc of haze,
but waves of light bending and speeding
as they pass from one frenetic sea of matter

to one more calm, then back again,
fervid clamor to hushed repose,
as if in stillness or at ease.

When Willebrord Snell sits by windowglow
in 1621, the canals boisterous outside,
the streets flowing, the sky a welkin sheet

streaked beyond despair
(scenes annealed by artists
in light that never darkens)

and dreams his law upon the page,
equations appear in black rows,
hymns of devotion,
in which luminous angels sing

of sensuous visions and glorious mirages
and the straight ways light flies blind
and then loses itself

in a world we know is real and unreal.
Like milk plunging braided
from a terra cotta pitcher,

plunging forever
in the hardened white lead
of paint.

Peasant Dance

He began with two steps forward
and one back,
        a kind of peasant dance
that slowed his journey
        to the pace of breath.
First, he saw the clouds
        then gazed down at the earth,
the creatures that inhabit it
        and the roads with their jumbled footprints
leading all ways at once.
        A philosophical puzzle
where he spun around
        like the needle of a compass
smashed on a rock.
        So he followed his instincts
and the aromas of the next meal,
        the fragrance of love
and the freedom of forgetting.
        His lessons were simple
and tumbled from his mouth
        in words that filled the silence,
and in the silence
        he wanted nothing to end.

What Is Left

The tabula rasa of the day
        reveals its openness, a landscape
                in which nothing has been painted—

no white farmhouse at the end of a long drive
        through planted fields,
                no copse of oaks offering shade

or pond where flashes of silver streak
        to the surface and raptors swoop down
                to seize the shadows.

No piebald cows deep in their grazing.
        The shimmering air smudges
                what the heart wants

and high above, the clouds congregate
        and plot their journey across the sky.
                At what corner of the canvas

will they begin their sketch of heaven?
        Desire's slow progress
                is what points the way ahead

and nothing not arising from our wanting
        finds traction. I remember my first taste of wine
                and the longing to feel what lay inside

the grape's dark ferment. So when the girl
        whose pale eyes were like sea glass
                wiped the liquid from her lips,

held the bottle out to me and said,
        Now you, I wasn't surprised
                by its sour sorrow,

as if the vine's roots had reached down
        into a cavern and drawn their nourishment
                from silence and emptiness.

Still, I wanted more, a craving born
    from the sweetness I knew
        the fruit should give,

when all the tractors have ceased
    and from what is left
        after many crushings.

Reading Buber
> *All actual life is encounter.*   —*I and Thou*

Everything in the living world is connected
to everything else.
Just the appearances of things
are different.
The vast silver maple
that spreads its branches
over the yard so a cardinal
has a perch to sing from
is connected to the bird
in the deeper realm
of their ancient molecules
that existed long before
any of us learned
what our own voices
sounded like.
So the tree and the bird
are joined to me,
and also to the woman I love
who sits in her study writing a story
about another tree
and the artist who tried to paint it
long after it first drew life
from the earth.
Beneath my skin,
I am with her
and all I see, says Martin Buber,
as I read him
out here, on the porch,
embraced by his ecstatic words
and all that surrounds me.

Aubade

Five sparrows fight for their lives
        in the sway of branches
that spider up against the sky,
        the sun lifting in silent breaths

from lungs that are masked by darkness,
        like a garment woven from wheat
growing in our deepest sleeping.
        I've walked through those fields,

though no one has seen me,
        and kneeled down to smell the sweat
rising up from the wastes and rivers.
        The stillness there wonders who will hear it,

whose ears are attuned to its quiet.
        Maybe it's the neighbor's dog
sniffing its way to paradise
        in the rich grass and its dense growing,

roots and rot commingling in a dance,
        bodies stuck together in slow cadence
to their own sighing.
        What is this thing called breath?

Is it the sauntering spirit, lost
        on a long journey, that seeks shelter
inside us as the night bears down?
        How time drifts as if no one can see it.

And we can't, except by the way
        each of us leans towards its leaving,
as if bidding farewell to a lover
        who steals without speaking

out into morning's shadows.
        These are what the clouds are—
dreams of escape that linger too long
        and become visible to their dreamers.

Pas de Deux

In the film "45 Years," as the characters Kate and Geoff
struggle toward each other
       with the nuggets of love
they still carry in the secrets purses
of their hearts, their hands constellated by liver spots,
       Geoff's chest bisected by the trespasses
of surgery, and his mind afflicted by nostalgia,
a word invented in the 17th century to describe the anxiety
       mercenaries feel about maybe never returning home,
the nearly frozen memory of his first love
haunts his marriage as an impediment,
       the sun having melted the snow
from the deep fissure that claimed her
while they'd hiked in the Swiss alps
       and the discovery of her remains coming to him in a letter
delivered past the lush fields, waterways
and dense copses of Norfolk.

As I watched all this on the screen,
the gestures and facial expressions
       of the long-married couple
like the contractions and releases in a modern dance,
perhaps a *pas de deux* played out amidst acts of domesticity,
       the making of tea, eating dinner together
at the kitchen table, or in the ungainly choreography of sleep
smoothed over by time and recorded deep
       in the motor nerves of the body,
it came to me that the first moment
of everything we love
       is our home, that hearing The Platters sing
"When your heart's on fire" for the first time
is what we yearn for,
       as husband and wife dance to it 45 years later,
when smoke has gathered in their eyes and along their spines
from what has burned and is lost
       and never drifts away.

How Poetry Has Let Me Down

Time in the distance shivers
like she did stepping out
        in the mist-cooled morning,
or as anonymous wings flicker in their flight
to wherever they're going.
        Sometimes only movement makes sense,
as condensation drips
inside my window
        and the sleeping cat whistles
his high-pitched snores,
more Motley Crue than Monteverdi,
        his nostrils narrowed tunnels
through which life passes into him.
Why has poetry let me down?
        How to make music
from a musty world that only mutters
and snorts, or to see beauty in the blotched
        watercolor outside the window?
All this effort and time converge
while ignoring the heart,
        which stumbles forward on its own journey
surrounded by flesh
and keeping it alive.
        To be a poet is to live
in a perpetual state of unrequited love,
always exposed and reaching out
        then attending to the silence.

DUENDE

All that has dark sounds has duende.   —Manuel Torres

When you lie sleepless in darkness,
your mind a desert
and the page barren, unappeased,

remember that words are like sacred objects
left behind by a fleeing tribe.
Polished wood in the shape of a fox,

a copper ewer,
feathers bundled and tied with beads.
Blow off the dust,

set them on a table,
let them tell you what they know—
the hidden pathways

through the woods,
the bitter distillations
that make you swoon,

the throat sounds and wild dances—
as your lips part
and your legs tremble,

and your ears ache
from your own heartbeats
that drum and echo back

through the distant nights.
And when your blood
after its long journey

at last finds its way
to your fingertips,
who would have believed

that in the midst
of your most arid wandering,
blossoms, inky blossoms,

would root and burst forth?

Hogmanay, Edinburgh

Past the iron fence on Princes Street
and up the Mound to the pale clock
on the steeple of St. Giles,
the denizens of this old town stumble
in weaving druidic lines,

chanting half-remembered ballads and dirty songs
bleated and belched off key,
guttural greetings, *och ayes* and halloos,
and hiccupping the music
the earth might have made

when it was drunk from its own first rains,
becoming what Burns called the "dews distilled,"
a liquor so smooth
it makes the tongue purr, stretch
and prowl for more

beneath smoke spuming from breweries
in the malty midnight air,
brine riding in sheets of mist
above whiffs of rust and turf
and the sweat and perfume of "C'mon, lass"

as lovers fumble in alleyways,
their damp backs pressed against stone and brick,
then their first hard kiss, their first moans,
these falling creatures the church bell summons
shivering and blinking into the New Year.

Holiday Candle

Thank you for your kind gift
of a red candle in a glass holder.
I put it on the side table
between the heavy Tibetan prayer bells

that summon the mindful,
and the black Japanese box fragrant
with riverbanks and stillness.
I will light it if Christmas neglects to come,

or if February is too much,
each day a dank shaft
with its dead canary. Maybe
I will even roast a chestnut

over the little flame
and eat the sweet flesh shaped
like the brain of a robin
and scatter the bits of shell

in memory of all the dreams I once had
that flew away from me.
Or perhaps I will hide it
in the deep oak drawer,

beneath my father's frayed sweater
with the felt letter and the big shoulders
that made the moths delirious,
and his rumpled prayer shawl

still smelling of hair oil and Luckies,
and his leather phylacteries
balled tightly like fists
inside their battered green pouch,

and it will be a memorial, a *yahrzeit*,
amid the faint davening, the musty pews,
and it will show me the way
when I search for him

one more time but can't find him,
and then when I stumble
past the objects
to join him.

For Those Whose Lives Have See Themselves

I am returning without you from the place we went together.
—Sezen Arseven, survivor, Club Reina, Istanbul

      Welcome all who have traveled the long road
from where your deepest dreams began
in the wild ferment of sleep,
      or when profoundly drunk or stoned,
and walked out
with whatever heavy burdens you carried,
      your thumb outstretched and maybe
your other hand taunting death with a sign saying,
"Beirut" or "Aleppo" or "Istanbul,"
      looked at the reflection of yourself
in your lover's Ray-bans and asked
what it meant to see the world
      and break the bonds that held you
to a former life, if only you could name
the thick liquid in which you'd floated,
      assured by the certainty of the next day
and all the days to come.
I remember in a cheap hotel in Amsterdam
      where the pipes entered and returned
through wide, rough holes in the sheetrock,
watching a couple make love in the next room,
      ashamed that I denied them
their privacy, their fumbling intimacy.
Perhaps they watched us too,
      as we abandoned ourselves for a few moments
above the bustling canals
and in the cracked mirror bolted to the wall
      opposite our bed. Who knows
what became of them? Or any of us
who are left in crummy hotel rooms
      by those we desire,
or because of bullets shattering raucous dancers
in a nightclub. Sometimes clarity
      only comes with loss,
for it tightens the skin
that binds us to our own silhouettes
      and makes our shadows sharper, more distinct
in the sun, or disappear forever
in the darkening, unholy cities.

Above Tripoli

High above the sea, above
        the gulls and crumbling stucco
                of Tripoli,
we rode in rumbling silence.
           The vivid air was acrid
                with pine smoke,
the snow reached downward
        like a ragged glove,
                the mountains swelled
and our eyes went white
        with them,
                I tense with an anger
I am now too old to know
        and you, your face a mask
                almost as beautiful
as Lebanon, and like Lebanon,
        curling at the edges
                from approaching fire.
In Bsharri, I stepped away
        and followed a path
                where ice was sheathed by stillness.
You may think
        it was a dream—
                a blue door in a mountain,
a tall chapped man
        in faded turban
                and crossed bandoliers,
his eyebrows raised suggestively,
        his voice hissing
                his salesman's pitch,
his rough hand hooking
        at my mouth.
                But I remember even now
how when I had fled
        and was clinging to a cliff,
                the rock clenched into itself
and dense with cold,
        I vowed that if I lived
                I would hug the first flesh
I would see. Above the cliff,
        across a field of snow rising

                    to a plume of cedars,
a spotted dog drawn forward
            by a wing of breath
                        flew at me.
Like Adam
        in his first embrace,
                    I was pulled into the world
of blood, then
            into the whiteness
                        that covers blood.

Fingers

There were only five things he cared about,
and each one he'd assigned to a finger of his hand.
Movement, deployments—that was his thumb.
Intimidation, to be jabbed with his forefinger

into a weaker man's chest. The middle finger
was contempt. The next, anonymity.
His pinky was the diminutive world of insects
for which he reserved his wonder

and what compassion he had left.
In the shivering filaments of a spider's web,
he saw the remnants of his own heart,
and in a cockroach, the creature

that inhabits his dust.
Once, his hand had been free,
a tool for doing in his boyhood
what had brought him joy. It was a scoop

to pull him forward when he swam,
or the supple vise he used to throw a ball.
And, when he was a young man,
the thing he stretched out to touch

the velvet cheek of a girl he thought he'd loved.
But lying for hours in the desert, wounded
and uncertain who he was,
his hand had clenched as if it held the hand

of someone he knew he'd never see again.
Only the ants had kept him company
in his deep pain and wasting thirst.
They moved along his arm in ordered lines,

indifferent, dauntless and dumb.
The chaos and smoke that had brought him there
made less sense than ever
and he felt something inside himself die,

so elusive it seemed inconsequential—
like one of his fingers—
and obscure as the anger that kept him alive,
and also as the tenderness.

Road Prayers in Afghanistan

The country was near last night,
it huddled next to me and against me
on our common, tea-stained earth,
blew mutton and rice piquantly in my nose
and touched my foot with another
that was not mine.

Perhaps it was the driver's
whose truck had brought me here so slowly
roadside rocks still beckoned
in my sleep. Their veins exposed and dry
from the crumbling strain of days,
they marked my journey backward into sight.

All this in my head when the *baccha* called
and pulled me up and through the wooden archway
into scouring air,
to watch the prayers of Afghan men
grouped closely on several spots
not one on a level with the next.
They moved in practiced unison,

like an old machine in a rough whisper of worn parts.
Foreheads lifted from rock, turned right and left.
Their *shalwar kameez* were flags hoisted in the wind
as they rose and sank under the weight of widening sky
perched wing-like on their capped heads.
My driver like all the others was barefoot
on his mat (smaller than the blanket of a child)
and spoke in a rumbling chant scraped
from deep inside his chest:

The world has turned to light
and I breathe,
and there is still air in my tires
and chai boiling to sweet green or brown,
and there is bread to chew
and gas to fill the truck,
and my shoes are close by
and my bicycles still tied and pile high
for market in Kabul.

To think—it was blackness
when the boy's voice cried
(May he be blessed!)
and I had forgotten my eyes
in the warm dust of yesterday.
But the water that flows below
has washed away all
and I am clean, clean
in the light, and to the One
who holds and turns us to him
like we are stones.

So I imagined these thoughts
inside the litany of words and flapping cloth.
I washed my hands, swam face down
in the pool they made, saw the lapis sky cut
by jagged gold, and turned again to Afghan men,
who kneeled and bent once more into the earth,
all modesty forsaken
by their scored, upturned, presented soles.

Liberty

Far offshore from the Cretan village of *Agia Galini*,
Saint of Tranquility,
the crew and I haul up nets of squirming fish—
        red porgy, octopus, mackerel and sardines—
that we dump in a heap on the trawler's rear deck
then scrape apart and sort
        with slats ripped from wooden packing crates.
We squat on other crates as we work,
our shoulders hunched,
        the tips of our cigarettes glowing,
stars scaling a sky as black
as the thick coffee we've just sipped.
        At dawn, the rising sun makes
the distant hills smolder,
and a sea turtle the Greeks call *chelona*
        is captured in a net
from a deep place our own lungs can't take us,
and *Eleftheria*, Liberty ... Terry I call him,
        crushes the turtle's shell
with the heavy steel hook
of a gaffing pole, an act of rage
        I've never understood, and heaves
the bleeding creature back into the sea.
What's become of Terry in the past forty years?
        Is he still dancing, drunk on retsina,
swaying his hips to the wild notes
of the bouzouki playing on the radio
        in Demo's Café, as he grips a chair
between his teeth,
raises it overhead, then releases it to our applause
        as dishes smash in tribute
on the littered floor?
Or maybe he entered the dark waters of Lethe
        and was reborn up the coast
in the town of *Ierapetra*,
where clothed in the bright red of a rescuer,
        he trudges through the crashing surf
carrying a shivering Syrian child
in the net of his arms and delivers him
        not into the frigid, bubbling sea,

but onto the same coarse sand
where turtles struggle up to lay their eggs
    in the swirling and ravenous wind.

Touching the Unknown

It's morning in Bulawayo
        with civil war nearby
but peace for now

in the fragrance of maize and tobacco fields
        the evaporating dew exhales
into the vigilant air.

Time to leave a young friend behind,
        who took me in as I wandered the streets
of that alien and imperialist city,

passing the night until the bus departed
        for the Zambian frontier the next day.
Paths from her parents' house

led us down to a canal
        then back to a supper
of salty biltong, brown bread and beer.

The cool flatness of flagstones
        where we lay on our blankets
in front of the fire

and watched inverted geckos
        lounge against the ceiling
waiting for their own meals to fly by.

Janet with her plans to escape from a country
        where equality was blocked
and not even a caress

could cross that barrier.
        At the bus, she took my face
in her hands and kissed me

as if touching the unknown.
        But my own lips were clenched,
a visible tightening of the heart

that even now I can't forgive
    or understand.
In my mind, purple jacarandas shimmer

along the Highveld
    and the day hemorrhages dust
into a cloudless sky

that crosses what we can't—
    the borders that define us and hold us,
and keep us apart.

Morning Hunger

Why not in the icy clarity of morning,
each edge carved by the sun,
vibrating and pale as it comes into form—
a mud wall framing my view,
a rug woven crimson and black
in delicate balance
and the serrated, purple hills of the Rif,
hungry for words, for the vowels of prayer—
why not forget everything?

Easy in this voracious place
where dreams die fast, un-nested
by the search for food
before the dew dries,
dries so quickly in Morocco,
a sight glimpsed rarely by travelers
and this first time by me
as a sheen fading
from a hanging rug.

Sitting against the wall,
our hunger building,
we see the sheep collapse, as if
weighted down by a fullness
beyond itself, its tongue pushed out,
its eyes rolled back and white,
and my friend asks, *Is the sheep dead?*

I ask Mohammed in French, who in Arabic
asks his uncle the same,
and he a lithe brown shadow
with white turban ends flapping
beneath the turquoise sky,
raises himself and kicks the sheep,
which bleats its last, like a doll
pushed over on its side,

returning its message—Arabic
to French to English,
words melted and recast
in the metallurgy of the throat—

The sheep is dead.

For breakfast there is clotted goat milk,
sweet mint tea and discs of bread
fragrant with cardamom.
Syllables of praise rush past my ears,
are aspirated, fleeting and become
the cantorial droning of flies
spiraling in ecstasy above the sheep's eyes.

The Sow's Dance

Abundance gathers in gray clouds,
       is woven into constellations
            by swallows
and diminishes by waterfall
      to a heart-shaped pool.
            A sow floats through the air,
her ears flapping, her wide nostrils
      snorting wind currents,
           she undulates and whirls
like a dancer in Swan Lake.
      She has never felt so lovely
           wreathed in scarlet breath
exhaled from her heavy carcass
      and wrapped in a tutu spun
           from the mud of her fluttering trotters
but the wind, dust and water
      give body to her dream.
           Lying on the sharp grass
above the Ankhu River in Nepal,
      I dream with her, dance
           with her high above the ridge,
catch her thinning scent,
      leap in tights stitched
           from beard and belly hairs
graying downward into earth
      to a music marrowing from bones
           blown hollow by the knowledge
this journey will end.
      I outsoar the swallows
           and then fall back
upon myself in the cold,
      hard, splatting bodies
           of raindrops.

A Kind of Floating

His days are a limbo
between two darknesses.
      Grey before the sun lifts slowly
from its curved bed
then disappears hours later
      behind a shadowy hedge.
He feels the empty spaces
his heartbeats occupy like thoughts
      that are as illusory as vapor.
A kind of floating without the thick heaviness
of the ocean under him,
      or even the rushing currents
of the river he must cross, swirling
amidst the glistening solid rocks.
      His heart thuds its way forward
and somewhere in the distance
he knows it will stop.
      Perhaps in the next darkness
with its stars shedding ancient tears
that water the meadows of asphodel,
      where he will lay down among them,
open his eyes to the clouds and know
that he is their brother.

When I Fell in Love with Sara, My Daughter

We sat in the park, she just awake,
her eyes cast up toward
the dry August trembling of oak leaves,

a slant of pigeons drifting downward
with their claws spread
and a few looping purls of cloud.

Sara, I said, her name still new to me,
my teeth and lips not used to it,
and read to her from a fat book of poems

I fished from the stroller's blue pouch.
She looked at me so gravely, I thought,
her tiny lashes feathering the air

and softening the tumble of syllables
upon her. But those words were gifts—
the husks of seeds already falling—

and her eyes, they gave back,
leaves, wings, the lighting sky,
the warm brown earth,

the stilling wonder of naming.

Tibetan Dress

In Boudhanath, I found a tailor
who would make my daughter
a Tibetan dress, souvenir of black
without sleeves, tied at the waist,

ankle length or longer and dragged
through the dust as if supplicating
the distracted gods, or like a bridal train
that follows a woman as she carves her shape

into the droning, unforgiving air.
Beneath prayer flags flapping their hollow music,
we haggled for the price of wool and silk
and the striped aprons that married women wear,

layers of yellow mustard flowers, rhododendron
and the pale green of barley shoots sprouting
from the terraced fields.
In my wheel of photographs

Boudhanath is a two-eyed stupa
against a taut sheet of lapis sky,
in thrall to the crow's wings
and the shadows they cast in winter.

Or else blurred alleyways
opening to circles of melting light,
where women rise like wraiths of smoke,
in black and in striped aprons hazy

and shimmering, as if seen at dusk
across a deep valley after fields have burned.
And my daughter, regal in her own small dress,
her eyes spread wide like wings across her face,

points at one image glowing and says,
Look, daddy, it's me, seeing only
the apron and the light
and the dancing, graceful darkness.

The Book of Forgotten Geniuses

I can understand why the Egyptians
        wanted to be entombed
among the artifacts
        of their lived lives—
papyrus etched with a procession of signs
        that would never stop intoning
in the silence,
        a carved granite ball ready
to be hurled at enemies
        in the next world,
and mummified cats hushed
        of all but the memories
of their soft murmuring.
        But not all were rich, nor am I
and desire only to be buried
        with the 3 dollars I got
for shoveling snow
        when I was 10—thus initiating me
into the ancient procession
        of capitalists—the obscure poems
I composed with the youthful ferocity
        of Mozart, a few amulets of grace
I carried back from the deserts,
        and my favorite tome,
The Book of Forgotten Geniuses,
        which like the *Chronicles,*
traces our journey from birth
        to the exile from which
we've never really escaped,
        and I shall gift it to Einstein, who
has rested all these years
        among his own relics—
the frayed bow of the violin he played
        to scratch out the music of his longings,
and the deflated tire of the bicycle
        he pedaled from the beginning
to the end
        then back again,
and with his thumbs still dusty
        from the chalk he used
to sketch his hieroglyphs about time

      onto boards as black
as the endlessness of space,
          he will turn the tattered pages,
slap his forehead in disbelief and mutter,
      "How come I
never thought of that myself?"

What I Want

Whatever I'm looking for now
is not within
a woman's body,

nor outside the skin of stars,
nor beneath
the ocean's flesh.

Nor is it encrypted in memories
annealed on old postcards
carrying strange stamps,

or whispering
from aerogrammes
as they flutter their pale blue fingers

bearing hieroglyphs
from the past.
What I do want

is the sharp solidity of stone
quarried from cliffs
and extravagant mountains,

where rain comes as snow
that covers, then expunges, the past
and glaciers embrace

then withdraw
from the earth.
I want rain like good whiskey

that falls again on my tongue,
which, haltingly, once more
begins to sing.

As a former Executive Director of The Writer's Center in Bethesda, Maryland, one of the largest literary centers in the USA, Stewart Moss helped establish creative writing programs for adult immigrants and members of the military being treated for neurological and psychological trauma. Prior to that, he worked as an educator and fundraiser in educational institutions around the country. He has taught literature and creative writing in both the USA and abroad; Scotland, Greece, Zimbabwe, Afghanistan, and Nepal are among the countries in which he has lived and worked. Moss has essays included in *Retire the Colors: Veterans & Civilians on Iraq & Afghanistan,* ed. Dario DiBattista (Hudson Whitman/ Excelsior College Press, 2016) and *Plume Literary Journal,* and poetry in *Plume, Goss183,* and *Origins Literary Review.* He has also been featured in "The Poet and the Poem" podcasts at The Library of Congress. He was educated at Union College (NY) and Harvard University. A native of Boston, MA, he resides in Annapolis, MD.

www.ingramcontent.com/pod-product-compliance
Lightning Source LLC
LaVergne TN
LVHW041600070426
835507LV00011B/1223